The Copywriting Laws: 50 Tips & Strategies to successful Copywriting

I0477066

By George Lucas

Table of Contents

CHAPTER 1

INTRODUCTION TO COPYWRITING

Copywriting is the workmanship and study of composing copies (words utilized in website pages, advertisements, limited time materials, and so forth) that sells your item or benefit and persuades imminent clients to make a move. From various perspectives, it's similar to employing one sales representative to reach the majority of your customers. A business group contacts clients each one in turn; a copywriter reaches all customers in one go through bulletins, magazine advertisements, direct mail advertisements, blog entries, and so on.

Whether you're a little entrepreneur, a medium-size entrepreneur, an eBay merchant, or primarily attempting to break into the copywriting business, understanding the essentials of composing deals situated copy puts you on a way to achievement. At its center, copywriting is another gadget in a business' promoting tool stash. Elegantly composed copy can represent the deciding moment for a commercial or showcasing piece. On account of that, copywriting can liken to either well-spent promoting ventures or a misuse of publicizing dollars.

Numerous individuals confound the uniqueness of compelling copywriting. I can't remember the number of times I've heard independent writers say they need to move from article writing to copywriting as though it's essentially an augmentation of their current capacities.

Copywriting does fall into place without a hitch for a few individuals, yet for most, it's a remote scene they don't know how to explore. Copywriting is about more than composing the hard undercut direct mail advertisement that numerous copywriting courses offer. Indeed, I flinch when I see those over-the-top direct mail advertisements, which do minimal more than give a monstrous representation of copywriting, deals and showcasing.

Copywriting, which is well created, doesn't have to beat a man over the head. It doesn't need to suffocate in striking typeface and promotion. The message ought to remain standing all alone without an excess of awkward deals, dialect and outline embellishments. I relate numerous direct mail advertisements that are liable to this procedure with an essayist who doesn't comprehend the essential reason for copywriting.

Fundamentals of copywriting

In case you're new to copywriting, you may feel overpowered by the greater part of the publicizing mediums you're figuring out how to compose. Whether you're hunting down an occupation as a promotion office marketing specialist or an independent publicist, these five publicizing fundamentals give you a prolog to copywriting.

1. Print Ads

Invest some energy finding out about print advertising. When you comprehend what makes a print notice compelling, you can move into learning about other print mediums like flyers, business catalog promotions, and pamphlets.

Composing print advertisements is likewise a simple approach to making tests for your portfolio.

2. Handouts

Don't simply take a seat and attempt to compose a pamphlet. Take in the essentials, for example, how the leaflet fits into the purchasing procedure if the handout will remain solitary or be tied in with other promotion mediums and what the offering focuses will be. Become acquainted with the five sorts of leaflets and you're headed to making an effective pamphlet.

3. Post office based mail

Composing post office based mail develops your new learning of composing leaflets. Standard mail is not one particular bundle of materials. As it were, not every post office based mail package is the same. Some may incorporate a direct mail advertisement and reaction card. Others may include a direct mail advertisement and leaflet. Getting acquainted with standard mail helps open you to a side of promoting that a few offices have practical experience in solely. This can be precious information to have in the event that you find you appreciate composing regular postal mail.

4. Advertisements

TV ads help you figure out how to compose sound to match the headline.

Making a: 30 TV advertisement script is a superb lesson in copywriting. Your script needs to time out splendidly, and you fuse sound and function with your duplicate and you additionally find out about the utilization of textual styles, design and different impacts in the business. This is additionally a decent time to learn about radio ads while you're in business mode. You can utilize both TV and radio advertisement without much of a stretch as composing examples for your portfolio as well.

5. Sites

Figuring out how to compose duplicate for sites is an absolute necessity for publicists. Indeed, even organizations that don't offer items online need a place so having and keeping up a site is something each group ought to be doing as of now. This is the place you, as a publicist, come in. You can likewise utilize site duplicate as a SPEC AD for your portfolio.

As an essayist working solely on the web, I'm frequently hesitant to urge others to take a stab at copywriting on the off chance that they don't comprehend the online commercial center. I can't let you know how regularly I've been told, "Goodness! I want to compose – I wrote impressive essays in English class!"

After an erratic grin, I am compelled to let the future essayist realize that composing copies for the web is in no way like composing an article for English class. Indeed, it's practically the inverse.

English expositions are intended to train, much like an instructor converses with a youngster.

Web duplicate is designed to connect with a crowd of people. You make a bond and discover shared encounters that a reader can identify with. This amiable nature regularly makes composing less formal and substantially more captivating.

Print duplicate, except for highlight articles and sentiments are frequently dull. They illuminate and educate. Web copy draws in, teaches and regularly prompts an extreme result. There's no "simply the actualities" here – the certainties fill a need, and that reason attempts further bolstering your good fortune.

Notwithstanding the composing you're doing with web duplicate, you have to remember how the readers are drawing closer it. Print shows up in daily papers, magazines, and books. Online copy is presently accessible through telephones, PCs, and tablets. The way content appears on the screen is distinctive. Finding out about page breaks and monitor measure, as well as text style dividing is all basic in helping guests actually read what you've composed on the web.

In case you're going to try out copywriting, remember a couple of things;

a.   Target Your Audience

Composing for the web means you're keeping in touch with somebody. Before you begin your venture, know who that somebody is. Propelled publicists know how to tailor their methodology for diverse gatherings of people – kids, high school children, ladies, men, retirees, housewives, youthful single men, whomever.

All that you compose is coordinated at your gathering of people, and they ought to know you're conversing with them. Utilize immediate, clear dialect to interface with your group of onlookers. Utilize "you" – there is no "one" or "certain people" in the web copywriting. "You" MUST be there, generally by what method will your gathering of people know you're conversing with them?

b. Clear Organization is Vital

Since your reader is in all likelihood skimming what you're keeping in touch with, you have to help control the eyes. Utilize any number of signs to demonstrate to your reader what's truly critical:

• Bullet focuses separate thoughts into nibble estimated pieces.

• Subheadings let you square particular thoughts together.

• Short square sections outwardly separate content.

• Bold words and expressions draw the eye.

• Different estimated textual styles make words bounce out at your reader.

Before you compose, plan what you're going to say. In the event that you think about your subheadings first and foremost, you can fill in the points of interest of every classification as you compose. This keeps you from being tedious or meandering.

c. Utilize Color to Attract Attention

Various studies have demonstrated that we see more and recall things better when they show up in shading. In the event that a particular expression is vital to your general message, make it bold by the use of alternate textual style shading.

Your objective is to draw the eye and make the message stick in the psyche of the reader. What preferred approach to convey it over in striking shading? A highly contrasting approach is so cool.

d. Compose Information Backwards

In one respect, a great bit of web duplicate is similar to English paper. You're going to tell the gathering of people what's most vital first. Tell your audience the primary thought in clear dialect. At that point go on and give him the subtle elements utilizing shots and engaging subheadings. Finally, wrap it up with an activity venture. For example, 'Click here' to take in more or 'Buy now!'

e.   Use Active Language

Your language ought to be pure and educational, yet with identity. Abstain from exhausting, aloof dialect for a dynamic voice. For instance, it's much better to say "Round out the structure underneath for extra data" than to say "Extra data will be sent after our receipt of the finished structure."

f.   Incorporate SEO and connections easily

Continuously compose for your readers – and those are the ones who can observe your nationality through your composition. Your sentences and thoughts ought to be clear, yet you ought to additionally pay consideration on the elephant in the web room – the web crawlers. In the event that you need readers to discover and read your work, you have to join the words they would ordinarily look for. These are the decisive words that you ought to work into your article wonderfully.

Use normal expressing and work essential words in with no cumbersome stating or degraded reiteration. While you're working indecisive words frequently, make certain to work with connections the same way. When you connection out to another site, abstain from utilizing the full connection or the name of the online production. Make the connection content portray what the connected page is relevant for. Case in point, in the short passage underneath, we'll focus on the watchword "Republican competitors" for SEO purposes and incorporate a power connect also.

The late civil arguments have demonstrated the expansive field of Republican applicants competing for spotlight paving the way to the 2012 race. With undeniable public cases beginning six months prior to the first essential race, it's safe to say Republican applicants mean business or are attempting to seem as though they do. Actually, the Wall Street Journal as of late added to the hypothesis encompassing the clothing rundown of Republican hopefuls by scrutinizing the purpose of Texas representative Rick Perry – will he be the following presidential possibility to enter the conflict?

g.   Guide Your Reader with Information

Use data to lead your reader to the right conclusion – he ought to tap into the connection, or she ought to feel a mind-boggling yearning round out that frame for more data. Your objective will be diverse relying upon the kind of business you're going to your site.

In case you're attempting to offer a top of the line administration, such as progressing SEO departments or sites through a Chicago web configuration organization, you'll take an altogether different methodology than in case you're attempting to offer a digital book or offshoot item.

h.   Consider Images

Web duplicate is a visual creature. Readers like to see pictures of flavor things, however, you must be mindful so as to utilize the right images. Unless you're doing a photograph diary section, your photos ought to supplement your content – they shouldn't overwhelm it. Think about utilizing as a picture close to the top, or "over the break" to attract the target group enthusiasm with the visual. Another picture about mostly down in the content is another extraordinary visual break also. Simply make sure that the image you select is one that supplements that partition of the material.

i.   Revise

At long last, it's discriminating to comprehend than even the best essayist commits errors. Continuously change your work and roll out improvements to enhance your duplicate. In the event that you don't see the outcomes, you'd like, adjust the content. Make it clearer or more coordinated to your group of onlookers. Duplicate is a living work – it can only change, and regularly it ought to.

CHAPTER 2

COPYWRITING TIPS FOR EFFECTIVE ONLINE MARKETING

It is quite tough to consistently produce high quality and powerful copy with the frequent demand for more quality content and increasingly growing need for effective copywriting. The need for quality copy is usually to attract visitors and convert them to leads and customers. The following points will enable you to avoid burnout, and get more results in the long run.

1.   Research, Research, Research!

All the great copywriters appreciate the value of research. David Ogilvy who is known as the father of advertising stated that writers should stuff their minds with information, so that they have plenty to work with. A legendary copywriter Gary Bencivenga was one of Ogilvy's students. He said that "the best copywriters are the most tenacious writers. They dig, drill, chip and dynamite like miners till they possess carloads of valuable ore. He continues to say that David Caples once advised him to collect interesting information that is seven times more than he could possibly use. The infallible cure for writers is research. More information enables you to have access to more possibilities that you can play with.

2.   Make it interesting;

In case you have no idea about what to write next or how to better your draft, one hint of copywriting is to add interest. David Ogilvy once said that in writing, you should tell the truth but make it more interesting. You don't want to bore people into buying your product. The only thing you can do is to interest them into buying it.

So the question is, how do you make your copy more fascinating?

• Ensure it is readable and appealing to the eye.

• Use your unique selling proportion or distinct personality.

• You can make it more entertaining so long as the humor you add will further your goal.

• Include controversy

• News jack

- Tell stories in your copy.

3.   Put a dose of personality

Each writer, as well as every brand has a unique voice, unique selling proportion and style. According to Ogilvy, building a sharply defined personality is often more effective in differentiating yourself from competition. It helps you gain a bigger market share. Before taking the next step to publish your copy, ensure that is is clearly demonstrating the personality of your brand. This includes your choice of words, style of writing , values, voice and USP. Your copy should also match the needs and desires of your target audience.

4.   Write a killer headline

David Ogilvy further states that five times more people read the headline compared to the body on the average. Writing your headline is like spending eighty cents out of your dollar. The body is only 20 cents. David Ogilvy and John Caples have written whole chapters on crafting powerful headlines in their copywriting and advertising books. The following tips will help you craft a powerful headline and subject lines to get you started;

•   Start with writing your copy, and then get the strongest phrases within your copy to use as headlines and subheading. This will go a long way in ensuring that your headlines are in match with your copy.

•   Go for headlines that are simple and straightforward instead of tricky and clever ones.

• Take the 4 U's into consideration i.e. Urgent, Useful, Unique, Ultra specific.

• Let your readers benefit, then ensure that you deliver within the body copy.

• Paint a striking picture or invigorate an extraordinary feeling. These snatch attention and include hobby, and they can quickly pass on the most essential advantage.

• Use David Garfunkel's Shortcut Test: If you posted the feature and a telephone number as a classified advertisement, would it produce calls for enquiry?

Copywriting Hall-of-Famer John Caples partitioned fruitful headlines into three categories. He would say, the headlines in the third best category utilized interest, the second-best utilized news, and the best of all utilized the self-interest of the reader. He proposed that scholars "attempt to get self-enthusiasm into each headline" and "dodge features that only incite curiosity. Even curiosity alone is not always enough."

5. Make your content simple

Albert Einstein, a German theoretical physicist, said that if you are unable to explain it simply then it means you do not understand it well enough.

Making your copy simple does not essentially mean dumping the technical jargon or writing a comprehension of the level of a ninth-grader. It means ensuring that your message is clear and succinct so your intended interest group comprehends your offer and advantages as fast as could be expected under the circumstances.

Eugene Schwartz, a renowned copywriter, put it along these lines: "write to the brain of a chimpanzee, simple and direct."

6. Give your interest group what they need.

Gary Halbert, a copywriter, recounts an anecdote about the best points of interest an eatery could have. It wasn't extraordinary food, low costs, or a decent location. The key to any eatery's prosperity is the starving group. You begin with a group of individuals who have shown they are hungry, and afterward you fulfill that need.

You can't create their desire to eat; you can just feed and channel it. Extraordinary substance and copy gives your interest group precisely what they effectively need.

7. Tell a story in your copy.

A 26-year-old copywriting freshman sat down in 1926 to compose a promotion for the U.S. School of Music offering home-study courses for would-be musical performers. He could have utilized a straightforward advantage feature, similar to Master the Piano at Home in 30 Days – Without a Teacher!

Be that as it may, he didn't.

He burrowed deeper. He realized that mastering an instrument is diligent work, and that the genuine reasons individuals do it is to be famous, to win their companions' adoration and envy, and to find satisfaction. That marketing specialist understood the genuine result of the commercial wasn't a course or the capacity to play, however fame and joy. Considering that, he still could have utilized the excellent how-to advantage feature, for example, How to Be the Most Popular Guy of Any Party!

But he never did that.

He realized that basically portraying performers' prevalence wouldn't be sufficient. He wanted the headline to resonate candidly with prospects. He wanted to make a clear picture of a buffoon—the sort of individual nobody ever envisioned could play – who left his companions staggered astounded by his execution.

His feature was "They Laughed When I sat down at the Piano but When I Started to play!"

At that point he utilized a large portion of his whole ad space to recount the tale of individual triumph, alluring prospects into reading the entire commercial and giving them a dream of the potential outcomes.

The young copywriter was John Caples, who was enlisted into both the Copywriters Hall of Fame and the Advertising Hall of Fame in the 1970s. That notice he wrote in the '20s propelled his vocation and is still viewed as one of the mainstays of the copywriting field. It worked since it caught the attention of prospects, drew them into a world they frantically needed to be a piece of, and left them hungry for more. The story displayed the item as doing the majority of the diligent work of figuring out how to play and conquered the complaint that you require an exceptional ability to play (since even the jokester could do it).

8. Make your copy more appealing to the eye.

Leo Burnett is a successful advertiser. He created straightforward icons to symbolize product advantages, and qualities that were straightforward and easy to understand (for example, the Jolly Green Giant and the Pillsbury Doughboy). One of his guidelines of copywriting was to "make it welcoming to take a look at" – since if the advertisement didn't welcome and seduce the eye, nobody would read it.

The same is considerably all the more genuine today, with the surge of content on the web, reducing the spans of attention-skimming readers. In the event that your substance doesn't have what David Garfinkel calls "eye claim," it won't get read or shared.

So how would you give your duplicate eye claim?

- A decent type font that is simple on the eyes and sufficiently enormous to read

- Short sections

- Assortment in the content, e.g. bolding, stressing, underlining

- Bulleted or numbered records

- Indented sections or quotes

- Headings and subheadings

- Visual signals, i.e. bolts indicating at the stress word

9. Try not to be shrewd.

As journalists and substance advertisers, we like to play with our words. Some of the time that is alright, contingent upon your image identity and the sort of material. However, being clear and compact will return more noteworthy prizes than being cunning in most instances.

As million-dollar publicist Gary Bencivenga said:

"Compelling copywriting is persuasiveness in print, not cunning wordsmithing. The more self-destroying and imperceptible your offering aptitude, the more compelling you are. Publicists who hotshot their aptitudes are as insufficient as anglers who uncover the snare."

10. **Break the guidelines.**

This copywriting tip may appear to be outlandish; however, the best authors know when and how to break the standards of fitting language structure, punctuation, and mechanics. As David Garfinkel said, "I've prompted numerous customers who feel constrained to utilize 'suitable English' in their direct mail advertisements... to 'flame your English educator!'"

Talking straightforwardly to your prospect in a dialect they'll effortlessly comprehend constantly more essential than composing things by the book.

11. **Keep a swipe document.**

A standout amongst copywriting indications that are understood the most is to keep a swipe file—a gathering of messages, promotions, and other duplicate or substance you adore or that performed well. That way, at whatever point you're stuck on an intense feature or don't realize what to attempt next, you can look through your accumulation and kick off your imagination.

12. **Have a reason behind all that you compose.**

With the substance advertising blast, loads of advertisers make content for content's purpose. Having a vast library of a substance can be unimaginably helpful, however just if every piece has a reason and fits in the general arrangement.

As David Ogilvy said, "In the cutting edge universe of business, it is pointless to be an innovative, unique scholar unless you can likewise offer what you make." Witty, cunning substance independent of anyone else doesn't provide you any benefit. Verify your content draws in your gathering of people, fabricates trust, and energizes deals first.

13. **Stay away from diversion.**

Infrequently when you're stuck written work, the genuine guilty party isn't an absence of thoughts or words, yet insufficient time to give to the venture. In case you're experiencing difficulty, attempt this copywriting insight and profitability hack from Eugene Schwartz.

Initially, shut the entryway and kill your telephone. Close or sign out of email and social networking. Kill whatever number diversions as could reasonably be expected.

At that point sit your seat and set a clock for 33 minutes. The main things you can do amid that half hour are to consider the composition extend and get the chance to take a shot at it.

Keeping away from diversion in copywriting

At the point when the clock goes off, take a 10-moment break and rehash.

With this framework, Schwartz expounded for 3 hours a day, five days a week and turn into one of the most generously compensated publicists of the 1950s and '60s.

14. **Consider unheard of options.**

David Ogilvy said, "Ability, I accept, is well on the way to be found among dissidents, nonconformists, and revolutionaries." Don't be reluctant to have a go at something else and new, because it might conceivably work. Discover and structure associations with the Mavericks, dissidents, and revolts in your field and see what incredible thoughts may start. Unfasten your balanced point of view and permit your subliminal to make associations between ideas. That is the point at which you'll concoct the best substance and copywriting ideas.

15. Speak to your target audience

Ogilvy likewise said, "In case you're attempting to convince individuals to do something, or purchase something, it appears to me you ought to utilize their dialect, the dialect they employ consistently, the dialect in which they think. We attempt to write in the vernacular."

Talking in their dialect helps prospects become acquainted with, as, and trust you because they perceive themselves in your words. That helps you interface and manufacture associations with them, and all the more effortlessly influence them.

In case you're stuck composition, retreat and verify everything sounds the way your clients think. Place yourself in their shoes. Make yourself imperceptible. Not just will your duplicate improve the activity, yet escaping from your particular manner like this can jolt new thoughts and enlighten what ought to come next.

16. Concentrate on advantages.

Each awesome marketing specialist encourages different journalists to underline advantages, not includes:

• John Caples said, "The best features are those that engage the reader advantages."

• Eugene Schwartz said, "Discuss what your item 'does,' not "is" – and exhibit this."

• Bob Bly said, "Basically all useful duplicate examines advantages."

Everyone discusses this copywriting tip because it meets expectations, and it is a moderately simple fix if your present copy isn't doing as such well. Make each element you say prompts an advantage.

17. Make prospects feel like they're now getting something.

Another excellent tip about copywriting from Schwartz is to make delight quick. At the point when prospects get something significant from you just by understanding, they figure out how to trust you and accept that you convey what you guarantee. This copywriting trap gives prospects a taste with the goal that genuine longing energizes their activities, not merely interest, and its additionally one of the reasons substance showcasing works so well.

18. Make inquiries that get readers to say "yes."

An excellent influence procedure utilized by Socrates and utilized auto business people, this hypothesis expresses that the more regular you can get prospects to say "yes," the more probable they are to say "yes" once more. A-rundown direct-reaction marketing specialist Parris Lampropoulos utilizes this strategy an alternate route: "In deals duplicate, I'll toss in an inquiry here and there, yet all the more frequently, I'll express it as an announcement. You know – one of those announcements that get prospects gesturing their heads."

In the event that they're stating "yes" and gesturing their heads, you've snared them.

19. Speak to the emotions of your target group

Right off the bat in his profession, Lampropoulos saw a specific copywriting gig as his opportunity to make it to the major alliances, so he did whatever is necessary. Notwithstanding was pressing it with verification components, testimonials, and value supports, he additionally "worked each conceivable feeling the reader may have." It was one of his best standard mail bundles, and it sent for a long time.

The trap to joining feelings in your duplicate is to ask yourself: what is my prospect's most profound yearning at this time? There are heaps of feelings you can engage, yet the key driving feelings – the most grounded, most intense feelings not represented by level headed thought – are:

• Fear

• Greed

• Guilt

• Exclusivity

• Anger

• Salvation

• Flattery

20. Attempt a one of a kind edge or snare.

At the point when approached about his procedure for composing stock stories and advancements for monetary pamphlets, Parris Lampropoulos said:

"First and foremost, I go to Fortune, Forbes and Business Week and read each article I can discover in the organization being suggested. At that point I do something bizarre: I take a seat and begin composing "interest" projectiles for those articles. Through this, I discover a broad range of unexploited deals points. Those points lead me to the "snare" for the stock story. Also, once I've got the snare, the story just about composes itself."

The web journals and magazines you take a gander at may be altogether different, yet the standard is the same: begin via looking into great sources, and then dig more profound to locate the distinctive, intriguing, strange, or unfathomable. Those brilliant chunks turn into the edge or snare you have to catch consideration and create interest.

21. Chase down the right words.

One of the most seasoned copywriting tips is to not utilize descriptive words and intensifiers to make an alright word sufficient. Find the absolute best word to pass on the message, feeling, or symbolism. It makes your duplicate more grounded, makes you as the essayist more undetectable so the readers can feel or see or comprehend what you need to pass on that vastly improved.

As Mark Twain broadly said, "The right word is the contrast in the middle of lightning and lightning bug."

22. Use Active voice.

More grounded and shorter than detached development, the active voice is less demanding to comprehend and passes on your message better and quicker. Passive voice makes you sound powerless, receptive or followed up on while dynamic voice assumes responsibility.

Case in point, the uninvolved sentence "More than 5000 clients have been helped by our administrations" is much more grounded in the dynamic voice: "We have helped more than 5000 clients."

23. Supplant "weasel words" with goals and guarantees.

Evading orders and solid words like "will" and "can" are a method for ensuring yourself, yet it makes you sound wishy-washy and not able to convey. Experience your duplicate and supplant each weasel word (e.g. may, trust, could, maybe, and so forth.) with the suitable basic or guarantee word (e.g. will, can, do, and so on.). This reinforces your duplicate and makes you sound sure, which constructs prospects' trust.

24. Move down your cases.

You'll sound significantly more sure and assemble more trust and validity when you demonstrate your case with dependable information. Move down your advantages and different cases with confirmation. This wins over cynic perusers and demonstrates that you truly do hear what you're saying. A couple copywriting thoughts to go down your cases may include:

- Facts and measurements

- Methodologies

- Testimonials

- Case studies

- Success stories

25. Use particular cases.

Resume scholars and school advisors instruct you to incorporate particular numbers in your resume on the grounds that they rapidly pass on your experience and abilities. This copywriting trap meets expectations in pretty much all that you compose, and it makes your duplicate more grounded by drawing in consideration and making you appear to be more sound – and vital. As Bob Bly, one of America's top publicists, says: "Since so much promoting is ambiguous and general, being particular in your duplicate separates it from different promotions and makes interest."

26. Assess your duplicate's proportion of "you" versus "we."

Successful substance showcasing and copywriting dependably begins with the client. That is the reason nobody needs to peruse leaflets or sites that just discuss the organization – and why duplicate that talks specifically to the prospect gets more results. When you verify your duplicate uses "you" in any event twice as regularly as "we" or your image name, you'll normally concentrate on your client's requirements and longings. Your duplicate will be more grounded, and you'll get more activity, leads, and deals.

Derek Halpern of Social Triggers is an awesome case. In his post about making stunning About Us pages, he discloses why it is imperative to incorporate an advantage driven feature-advantage driven presentation- and social evidence. To see his recommendation in real life, look at his Social Triggers About page. There's a ton of "I" and "Social Triggers" in there—but there's additionally huge amounts of "you." He talks straightforwardly to his group of onlookers so they know precisely what they can anticipate from him.

27. Fuse the basics of influential copywriting.

As per "America's Top Copywriter" Bob Bly, the basics of influential copywriting are:

- Gains consideration

- Focuses on the client

- Stresses advantages

- Differentiates you from the opposition

- Proves its case

- Establishes believability

- Builds esteem

- Closes with an invitation to take action

Contingent upon your item, prospect, and sort of substance, you will not have to utilize each of the eight. Case in point, built up brand names shouldn't stress over verification and believability. Yet, remembering them while you compose and reexamine can help you make more grounded, additionally convincing duplicate.

28. Use symbolism.

Symbolism helps readers immediately comprehend a circumstance or advantage (furthermore, it makes your duplicate all the more intriguing to peruse). Publicist David Garfinkel says one of his most loved features/mottos is this one for a pipes administration:

"Call Roto-Rooter – that is the name -

Furthermore, we're off inconveniences, down the channel!"

Depicting it, he says: "Wow – is that flawlessness in two or three lines, for sure? You get an invitation to take action, organization distinguishing proof, and a visual depiction of the advantage."

The symbolism of the channel in a flash passes on the advantage. It's additionally huge, dependably an or more in extraordinary substance.

29. Lead with your most grounded point.

Such a large number of scholars spare their most powerful focuses for last, when it ought to be the other route around. A larger number of prospects will read the starting than the end, so putting your best thought first is more enticing. The most grounded point can frequently get consideration better than weaker focuses, making it perfect for the starting.

30. Manufacture believability.

Another exceptionally fruitful publicist, Steve Slaunwhite, said:

"As far as I can tell, the most obvious key to influence is this: impart trust. In the event that you do this well, you at any rate have a chance at drawing in and influencing the readers. In the event that you don't handle this well, then again, no measure of extravagant copywriting methods will spare you."

You can construct believability and trust by saying accreditations like:

- Solid ensure, return, and protection strategies

- Testimonials and information about your reputation

- a long time in business

- advancements and recompenses

- distributions

- enrollment and investment in expert social orders

- seals of endorsement

- office appraisals

- autonomous review results

- media scope

31. Notice the most essential point no less than three times.

This is Winston Churchill's "colossal whack" hypothesis, which says to not be unobtrusive or sharp about your vital point. Richard Perry says, "Utilize a heap driver. Hit the point once. At that point return and hit it once more. At that point hit it a third time- a huge whack."

Effective journalists and advertisers utilize the force of three constantly.

Derek Halpern prompts putting a select in structure in three spots on your About Page.

Heaps of email advertisers incorporate three connections in an email to drive clicks (simply take a gander at a couple of the email bulletins you get).

Long-shape greeting pages frequently have three CTA territories.

In the case of something's critical, say it toward the starting, again in the center, and again toward the end.

32. Anxiety esteem.

America's top marketing specialist Bob Bly says, "It's insufficient to persuade prospects you have an extraordinary item or a prevalent administration. You should likewise reveal to them that the estimation of your offer far surpasses the value you are requesting it."

Demonstrating the general worth is otherwise called the "small detail within a bigger landscape" procedure, where the expense of procurement is a minor thing contrasted with the advantages your offer conveys. This works for email memberships and website remarks and in addition item deals, since perusers surrender something they value—their time, email address, privacy—to receive something of quality consequently.

This basic copywriting tip meets expectations truly well in conjunction with tip #17, giving momentary satisfaction. On the off chance that they as of now get esteem from your substance, the estimation of your offer is probably justified regardless of the expense.

33. Incorporate an in number invitation to take action.

In the event that you don't particularly request that individuals do something, odds are they won't do it. All that you compose, from blog entries to messages to social redesigns to points of arrival, ought to close with an invitation to take action (CTA). To get the most out of your CTAs, verify them:

- match the purchaser persona and phase of the purchasing cycle

- offer something of worth

- offer prospects something they really need

- repeat your most critical advantage or enthusiastic driver

34. Make it individual.

Marketing specialist David Garfinkel says that fruitful substance is close to home, and it doesn't utilize stilted formal English or "stickler" dialect of a school task. He prescribes writing in a more individual, loose style, as though you're having an one-on-one discussion with your prospect.

Examination shows that customized messages change over superior to anything mass messages, and most web advertisers realize that the best web journals utilize the casual, individual style.

35. Arrange your written work with an equation.

AIDA is a prominent direct mail advertisement design for a reason – it meets expectations. Utilizing a system like consideration interest-craving activity (or John Caples' adaptation, consideration interest-activity) makes it simple to know precisely what to compose next.

Here are a couple of different structures and equations to help you begin:

- Dan Kennedy's most loved copywriting equation is PAS, or Problem-Agitate-Solution. It meets expectations on the grounds that individuals are more inclined to act to evade torment than get pick up.

- Copy blogger advances a straightforward 1-2-3-4 structure that helps you concentrate on the client and fuse the most essential influence essentials.

- Essential copywriting recipes and agendas to make your duplicate as strong and powerful as possible.

CHAPTER 3

COPYWRITING METHODS

Copywriting is real convenient. When you do your study and prep work, your copy will shine. Don't be afraid to take calculated risks and be taught from your errors, however do not waste your restricted advertising price range. By using doing the legwork first and fully finishing your copywriting define, you'll have a working document you need to use as a tool to supply your entire copywriting projects now and sooner or later. Spend a while up-entrance to boost a primary expense copywriting define, and you'll be able to reap the rewards later with a boost in revenue and earnings and a larger return to your promoting investments.

1.   Make the most your product's benefits.

Step one of the copywriting is the foundation for your promoting campaigns. A advantage is the worth of your product to a customer. In different words, a improvement is what the product can do for a patron or how the product can help a consumer. You ought to put into phrases the causes your product is the fine to be had and better than your rivals' merchandise centered on the added value it presents to your consumers. The key to success is so that you can absolutely realize all the advantages of your product. Best then can you make certain that the viewers know them and might relate to them.

2.   Exploit your competition's weaknesses.

To put in writing compelling copy, it's primary that you recognize what differentiates your product from the competitors. Once you recognize your rivals' weaknesses, you have to make sure your audience knows them and is familiar with why purchasing your opponents' products would be a horrible mistake. Get began via completely researching your competitors and understanding what they offer in terms of merchandise and services. Subsequent, list the factors of their choices that are not so good as your possess. Suppose free to tear the competition apart but be sensible on your comparisons. You want to be ready to help your claims in case you are challenged.

3. Comprehend your viewers.

Every individual on this planet is just not going to check every ad on the earth. Every advert has a unique audience so as to see it, and it can be the marketer's job to find the first-class placement to make certain the goal audience will see it. For instance, an advert for skateboards placed in a nearby senior citizen housing association newsletter is not prone to generate various sales. In fact, it might be a waste of advertising dollars. The target viewers for skateboards are teens or younger adults. The mammoth majority of senior residents don't use skateboards, and it's not a product category where they probably purchase gifts. Before you purchase advert area, make sure you are spending your cash within the right position to get the largest bang to your buck in phrases of exposure and building awareness of your services or products.

First, take the time to research your consumers entirely. In most businesses, 20 percent of shoppers are responsible for eighty percent of revenue (that is called the 80/20 rule in case you're curious about the respectable advertising terminology for this phenomenon). That 20 percentages represents your great purchaser and your job is to examine who that 20 percent is. Evaluation your purchasers and put together a demographic profile of your most valuable client, so you could advertise within the satisfactory areas to find identical people who are doubtless possibilities. If you're a small trade owner, you most commonly don't have a finances put aside to conduct an intensive research be trained and evaluation of your patron base, so you'll be able to must improvise by way of utilizing your own communication expertise and visual investigation. Take into account; you're trying to increase a common profile of your goal purchaser, not a CIA profile of every man or woman who buys your product. Do your pleasant with the expertise you may have.

There are numerous attributes you should utilize to boost a demographic profile of your buyers. Following is a list of examples of qualities to aid you in starting your own demographic profiling initiative:

- Gender

- Age

- Ethnicity

- Household popularity

- Income

- Occupation

- Pursuits

4. Communicate W.I.I.F.M. (What's In It For Me?)

There is a sort of factors to create an advertisement or marketing piece. Earlier than you write copy on your promotional piece, you must realize your pursuits for that piece. What do you need to get in return? The reproduction you employ in each and every advert or advertising piece will fluctuate situated to your goals for that promoting. While this booklet does not focus on the progress of advertising and marketing plans and approaches, i will offer some examples of one of a kind ambition for commercials or advertising portions that, in flip, will impact the reproduction you utilize:

- communicate a specific present

- Share expertise and raise cognizance

- Generate leads

Your customers need to fully grasp how your product or service goes to aid them by means of making their lives less difficult, making them suppose higher, helping them save money, serving to them retailer time, and so forth. On this step of the copywriting outline, you'll construct on the work you've completed so far by means of taking your product's points, advantages, and differentiators and principally describing how they straight influence your goal audience members' lives in positive approaches. Bear in mind the primary tenet of copywriting-- your product or service is a ways less primary than its capability to meet your consumers' needs.

Reply your target audience's query "What's in it for me?" take into account; you are paying on your advert area and very likely picture design too. Don't waste your money via inserting an advert with ineffective replica that does not clearly tell your shoppers what they may get by buying your services or products. Enormous organizations with large promoting and marketing budgets can scan snappy, cliché headlines and replica in an try to in finding the fine way to capture their target viewers' attention, but small and medium-size business owners in most cases have confined budgets. For smaller companies that best have one threat to communicate their message, reproduction have got to be written so the message, including advantages and differentiators, is heard and understood by means of the goal viewers. There is not any room in a small trade owner's advertising funds to chance no longer getting that specific message throughout to the proper people whenever.

5.   Focus on "you," not "we."

it is essential that you are conscious of how you're addressing your patrons to your copy. To do this, you ought to have an understanding of pronoun utilization. Feel again to your school days. Bear in mind your English teacher explaining first individual, 2d person, and 1/3 person? As a refresher, first man or woman (I, me, my, mine, we, us, our, ours) is the man or woman speaking and 2d individual (you, your, yours) is the person to whom one is talking. It can be essential that you just write copy that speaks to your goal audience and no longer at them--and no longer about you. Consequently, the majority of your copy in any ad or advertising piece must be written within the 2d person. For example, do you pick copy that says, "by way of our first-class income department, we are able to supply automobiles within 24 hours" or "which you could power your new car day after today"? At the same time the primary copy example focuses on the industry, the 2d instance focuses on customers and speaks immediately to them. It's extra individual, and accordingly, extra mighty.

Bear in mind, writing in the second man or woman helps your viewers swiftly join the aspects for your replica to their possess lives and allows them to customize the advertisement or advertising and marketing piece. That is how the advert is attached to an individual patron's possess existence. By means of writing your copy so it makes a specialty of the client instead than yourself, the patron can customize the advert and product you're promoting and act therefore.

6. **Appreciate your medium.**

As you write your copy, be mindful that each extraordinary medium the place an ad is positioned requires another tone or sort. Relying on the place you're putting your advert, the replica you employ alterations founded on the audience who will see the ad. Are you inserting your ad in a nearby newspaper or on a billboard? Are you inserting your ad in a woman's magazine or in a information magazine? Distinctive media require distinctive replica to most easily persuade a distinctive viewers to behave. Moreover, exclusive forms of advertising and marketing pieces require one-of-a-kind forms of replica. Take into account, there are a lot of methods to use copy to advertise what you are promoting as opposed to common advertisements. Use every feasible and correct opportunity to communicate your advertising messages to your purchasers.

7. Avoid Too Much Information

You should by no means risk shedding the attention of your audience by offering too much information in your copy. Amazing copywriting tells your viewers what they must understand to act and make a purchase order or the best way to contact you for more expertise. Extraneous small prints muddles the minds of your viewers, which increases the possibility of them forgetting the foremost points of your commercial or advertising software. Except you are advertising a prescription drug, tremendously technical gear, or an tremendously regulated or tricky product, the satisfactory rule to follow is "keep it simple, stupid". You're spending a large amount of your advertising funds on placing every ad. With every ad, you best receive a small amount of house to get your message across to your audience. Accurately use that costly real property to make sure you get the perfect return for your investment.

8.   Incorporate a call to action.

The goal of any ad or advertising piece is to elicit some style of response from the audience who sees it. A name to motion is the detail of replica that tells an viewers how you need them to reply to your commercial or marketing piece. Normally, the call to action creates a sense of urgency round a message and presents guidelines on what to do subsequent. For example, a name to motion might inform the audience to call the advertiser or talk over with their retailer or internet site.

Including a call to motion is with the aid of a long way the most important part of potent copywriting. It is essential that you are making it convenient to your audience to act to your ad or marketing message. You already persuaded them to need your product with the aid of following Step 1 by means of Step 7 of the copywriting define and by means of writing influential copy. Now you must ensure your audience can respond simply to your advert and buy your product by means of compelling them to act.

To, ensure the sentence constitution of your copywriting is in an active rather than passive voice. The reason for this is easy. Reproduction that you simply write within the lively voice is with the aid of definition motion-oriented, while replica that you write within the passive voice talks concerning the motion in a faraway manner. To extra explain, while you write a sentence in the lively voice, the field of the sentence performs the action of the verb in the sentence. However, if you write a sentence in the passive voice, the field of the sentence receives the action from the verb of the sentence.

The second step in developing an amazing name to motion to your copy is constructing a way of urgency. Your purpose in advertising is to create consciousness of your product or service and, eventually, increase revenue. When do you want to do that? Do you wish to have your purchasers to act tomorrow, subsequent month, or next 12 months? If you are spending cash on promoting now, you surely want your shoppers to behave now. If that's the case, your replica wishes to inform them to get off the sofa and get into your retailer now. There are a lot of words and phrases which you can add to your reproduction to create a sense of urgency.

9.   Cover your weak point

Whilst large companies have authorized departments that evaluate reproduction to be certain it does no longer expose the enterprise to knowledge problems, smaller firms don't often have the budget to seek the opinion of an attorney for each ad they run or advertising piece they print. Nevertheless, that does not mean small trade house owners have any less responsibility for producing advertisements and advertising pieces which are sincere and not regarded misleading. Most small trade homeowners are sole proprietors which means, if they lose a lawsuit, now not best can their trade assets be used to satisfy a plaintiff's demand, however their private belongings will also be distinct as well. When you're writing replica, bear in mind if claims that you just are not able to show for your copy (or are not able to provide correct disclaimers for) are worth it while you weigh the risk vs. the expertise reward.

Except for opening yourself up to feasible litigation, exaggerating or falsifying claims about your product or your competitors is unethical and a nasty trade observe. If you're caught in a lie (irrespective of how small it is), word will spread quickly, and your status could be irreparably broken. Once more, weigh the danger vs. the capabilities reward earlier than you advertise utilizing claims you cannot show.

Be careful of using phrases superlatives such because the examples within the following record:

- Free

- assured

- Quality, lowest, quickest, etc.

- Or your a reimbursement

- secure

- No threat

- No buy crucial

- No rate

- No obligation

- No funding

- A hundred percentage

- Promise

- No questions asked

10. **Proofread.**

It is vital that you competently proofread your reproduction. One of the crucial quickest approaches to lose credibility in promoting is to allow grammatical or spelling errors to appear on your advertisement or advertising pieces. Shoppers translate carelessness in ads into carelessness in products and repair. They ask themselves, "If this enterprise would not care ample to supply an advert without errors, how likely are they to care about caring for me?" reliable corporations produce respectable pleasant advertisements and ad reproduction, and that means their reproduction has been proofread over and over and is error free.

It really is that simple

CHAPTER 4

WHAT TO DO WHEN YOUR COPY IS PLAGIARIZED

Whether you've put time and vitality into composing your own substance or contracted an expert publicist, discovering your copy on another person's site is irritating. There are individuals who think that in the event that it's on the Internet, then it is free. Some don't even try to change the organization name or business-particular data. Yet, you can put a stop to it!

The Internet makes it simple to catch the culprit before the encroachment harms your notoriety or your web search tool rankings (an excess of locales with the same substance can bring down the greater part of their rankings or reason them to be uprooted).

Do you know the rights you have for securing your site content? "One thing individuals don't know is the point at which they have copyright rights. You can't uphold your rights if you don't have any acquaintance with them. Individuals ought to attempt to advise themselves. Check the administration. Check nearby sources. Regularly there are courses on different regions of the law," clarifies Jasmine Abdel-Khalik, Associate Professor of Law at University of Missouri-Kansas City.

Obviously, the data gave here is not expected to supplant the counsel of an expert lawyer. In any case, it can help you find whether your site duplicate is being copied and offer recommendations to practice your copyright rights under the law.

How would I know whether somebody is copying my site content?

There are two speedy approaches to check whether your site substance is posted on another site. Sort your URL into a counterfeiting checker like Copy scape or copy and paste parts of your most interesting sentences into Google.

In the event that your site is the stand out that makes a mockery of, your substance is ok for the time being. Be that as it may, if different destinations show up in the list items, tap on those showing your substance to see precisely how your copy is being utilized. Once in a while it might be a matter of connecting to yours and it is referred to appropriately. The more connections back to your site can enhance your site's web index rankings, particularly on the off chance that it is a mainstream website.

What steps would I be able to take in the event that somebody is utilizing my site content?

Utilize the data on the contact page as your beginning stage. In the event that there is no contact data, take a gander at the footer segment for a website admin address or facilitating organization. Send a decent message asking for that the substance be evacuated and where the first duplicate is found. Some site proprietors don't have the foggiest idea about the substance is appropriated and are the unknowing casualty of a corrupt publicist in their own particular promoting office.

As far as I can tell, this first email generally deals with the issue. Now and again an expression of remorse email is gotten and infrequently the substance just vanishes from the site. Keep in mind to catch up after the first email is sent and even a couple of months after the fact to verify your copy do not return.

In the event that that doesn't work, sort in the space name at Whois.com. The proprietor's name and telephone number ought to show up in their records. Contact the site proprietor straightforwardly to demand prompt evacuation of the appropriated substance.

On the off chance that that fizzles, illuminate the site's facilitating organization of their customer's copyright encroachment. Facilitating organization data is found on the Who is site under the area enlistment data or now and then on the site itself. When it is affirmed that the substance is in infringement, some facilitating organizations will uproot the site instantly.

Still no reaction? You may think about mailing as a formal "Stop this instant" letter. Your lawyer can help you with the fitting configuration since the wording may influence your rights in the event that it goes to court or you can scan the web for cases. Send it ensured mail.

A conceivable final resort? Exercise your rights under the Digital Millennium Copyright Act (DMCA). You can go straightforwardly to the significant web search tools like Google and Yahoo with your copyright encroachment objections.

I didn't legitimately enlist my site duplicate. Do despite everything I have copyright insurance?

Whether you recorded the enlistment research material or not, your web content is still ensured by Copyright laws. Copyright assurance starts right now of creation in a substantial medium and whether its distributed or unpublished.

How would I demonstrate my site substance existed first?

You can check the Internet Archive Way Back Machine to see when your webpage was initially listed with that substance contrasted with the other website being referred to.

What does the copyright enlistment procedure include?

Enlisting your site substance can be as straightforward as rounding out an online enlistment frame and paying a charge, as meager as $35. You can discover all data and structures on the authority U.S. Government Copyright Site.

Does every page should be enrolled independently or would I be able to enlist the whole site?

I have had customers do both. Case in point, a land master copyrighted both his website content and a broad downloadable migration guide. Counsel a copyright lawyer to see which decision best secures your substance and hobbies.

On the off chance that my copyright assurance naturally starts at creation, why try enlisting it?

Legitimate enrollment is obliged in the event that you ought to need to make lawful requirement move by suing in court. Early enrollment may permit you sue for more statutory harms. Copyright cases must be recorded on the government level.

As per the U.S. Government Copyright site, "Enrollment is suggested for various reasons. Numerous decide to enroll their works in light of the fact that they wish to have the truths of their copyright on general society record and have an authentication of enrollment. Enlisted works may be qualified for statutory harms and lawyer's expenses in fruitful prosecution. At last, if enlistment happens inside of 5 years of production, it is viewed as by all appearances confirm in a court of law. See Circular 1, Copyright Basics, segment 'Copyright Registration' and Circular 38b, Highlights of Copyright Amendments Contained in the Uruguay Round Agreements Act (URAA), on non-U.S. meets expectations."

Does my site have copyright security against global encroachment?

The U.S. has corresponding concurrences with numerous nations. In any case, your level of assurance relies on upon what that specific assertion states and who marked it.

CHAPTER 5

LAWS TO ABIDE BY TO AVOID LEGAL BACKLASH

Law has been everywhere throughout the advertising news recently. Initially, there was the entire SOPA/PIPA dramatization. What's more, you may have additionally seen that protection has been truly a hot catch issue as of late, with the dispatch of Google's new one-size-fits-all security arrangement and the most recent failure with the best in class (or perhaps not?) informal organization, Path . With such a great amount of laws overseeing the web, as an advertiser, you may be considering how it could influence the way you carry out your employment.

So in the event that you need to verify you're not being an advertising criminal, this is what you have to know regarding the significant laws that apply to advertisers so that you don't end up with a court case or worse. Talk has it you can't blog routinely in the slammer.

1.   CAN-SPAM Act

The CAN-SPAM Act (or the 'Controlling the Assault of Non- Solicited Pornography And Marketing Act of 2003') is a law that diagrams rules for business email, sets up prerequisites for business messages, furnishes email beneficiaries with the privilege to make you quit messaging them, and lays out huge outcomes for infringement of the Act, (for example, punishments of up to $16,000 for every different email infringement). As an advertiser, the majority of your email showcasing messages need to consent to the necessities put forward in the CAN-SPAM Act.

Instructions to Abide:

• Avoid utilizing misdirecting, beguiling, or adulterated data in your "From," "To," "Answer To," title, and steering data. Verify you unmistakably recognize who is sending the email, whether it is from an organization or a person. Verify your email headline obviously demonstrates what the substance of the email is about.

• Include your physical postal location. Each email message you convey needs to incorporate your legitimate physical postage information.

•   Include a quit connection, and honor unsubscribes expeditiously. You must incorporate a reasonable and clear route for beneficiaries to unsubscribe from all email correspondence from you, regardless of the fact that you likewise give a rundown of different sorts of email to which they can subscribe. In the event that a beneficiary requests that be expelled from your rundown, you must respect their solicitation inside of 10 business days, and afterward you can't offer or exchange their email location to another rundown.

•   Choose a legitimate email administration supplier (ESP). Regardless of the fact that you're sending messages utilizing an ESP like Hub Spot

, that doesn't mean you won't be held obligated if the messages sent aren't consistent with CAN-SPAM regulations. Both your business and your ESP can be considered in charge of a screw-up, so verify you select an authentic ESP for your email advertising.

Genuine Offender: In 2004, Nicholas Tombros pled liable to charges and turned into the first spammer to be indicted under the CAN-SPAM Act of 2003 for " war-spamming " thousands with messages publicizing explicit sites. Tombros was sentenced to three years of probation, six months of house capture, and was fined $10,000.

2. Try not to Call Implementation Act

You've likely known about the National Do Not Call Registry, which permits U.S. customers to farthest point the telemarketing calls they get. This is the Act that got it going, and today, more than 200 million individuals are enrolled with the Do Not Call Registry. The Do Not Call Registry doesn't keep every single undesirable call, for example, calls from associations with which a man has set up a business relationship, calls for which a man has given former composed authorization, calls that aren't business or do exclude spontaneous ads, or calls from or in the interest of expense absolved non-benefit associations. Disregarding this Act will cost you up to $11,000 per infringement. Now that is a lavish telephone call.

Step by step instructions to Abide:

Here's the undeniable counsel: Don't frosty call! Utilizing inbound advertising to set up a business association with a prospect first spares you from being a slave to the Do Not Call Registry. In any event, limit it. In the event that you do icy call using telemarketing.

- Regularly upgrade your rundown. You're obliged to pursuit the Do Not Call Registry in any event once at regular intervals and expel from your call records the telephone quantities of new registrants.

- Do not call individuals on your rundown before 8 AM or after 9 PM. It's disallowed.

Genuine Offender: In December 2010, the FTC close down two gatherings of Florida-based telemarketers that immersed customers with "robocalls" in which they erroneously guaranteed to lessen purchasers' charge card rates. JPM Accelerated Services-related respondents were fined $5.9 million, and fines of $3.2 million were requested to six different litigants who were connected with a partnered operation, IXE Accelerated Financial Centers.

3. Security Policies and Terms of Use

Albeit incomplete regulations exist, there is no security law that without any help addresses how you can procure, store, or utilization individual information in the U.S. For the most part talking, in the U.S., whoever annoys with gathering information is considered to possess the privilege to store and utilization it. That doesn't mean you ought to play with flame. With the late cases of Google and Path, we've seen what happens with organizations when they're thought to have mishandled clients' close to home data. Besides, its additionally vital to comprehend other sites' terms of utilization in case you're utilizing them as a part of your promoting system. This is what you ought to do to remain focused safe side.

Step by step instructions to Abide by:

• Create a protection strategy and terms of utilization for your business. Make them plainly unmistakable on your site. In your security arrangement, verify you plainly convey how you utilize individual data, who you impart it to, and whether you utilize treats or following programming. In the event that you say you won't offer clients' data or email locations to different merchants, don't offer their data or email locations to different sellers.

•   Provide a connection to your protection approach on or close to your presentation page frames and in email showcasing messages. This won't just build up you as a valid, reliable seller, however it will likewise stifle nervousness, make less grinding, and therefore expand transformations.

•   Never offer or offer touchy data. This incorporates government disability numbers, MasterCard numbers, ledger data, criminal foundation, or wellbeing records.

•   Adhere to different sites'/business' terms of utilization. This is especially vital in case you're utilizing outsider online networking destinations in your promoting procedure. Verify you counsel these destinations' terms of utilization before you utilize them so you recognize what is and isn't adequate showcasing conduct on every individual site. Case in point, would you say you were mindful that Facebook has really strict rules about how you can run challenges and special battles on its site?

• If you direct business universally, get your Safe Harbor affirmation. Proposed for associations inside of the EU or U.S. that store client information, the Safe Harbor Principles are intended to avoid inadvertent data revelation or misfortune. US organizations can select into the system the length of they stick to the 7 standards delineated in the EU Data Protection Directive on the security of individual information . For more data, visit the official Safe Harbor course of action site .

Genuine Offender: In November 2011, Facebook consented to settle government charges from the FTC that it damaged clients' security "by letting them know they could keep their data on Facebook private, and afterward more than once permitting it to be shared and made open." The settlement obliges Facebook to permit free examiners to survey Facebook's protection rehearses throughout the following 20 years. It additionally obliges that Facebook get approbation from clients before changing how it handles their information.

4. Slander Law

Defamation is a bogus proclamation of reality that is unsafe to somebody's notoriety and distributed as an aftereffect of carelessness or malevolence. Contingent upon state laws, slander is frequently characterized in particular ways. Defamation is composed criticism, though criticism is talked maligning. Fortunately, under Section 230 of the Communications Decency Act , sites are secured against stigmatizing client created substance, for example, web journal remarks, which implies you won't need to screen and get rid of that sort of substance (despite the fact that you'll most likely need to evacuate it in any case).

Instructions to Abide by:

•   Don't ill-use your right to speak freely in your substance. You have the privilege to impart your insights in your substance, however stay away from conclusive proclamations that out and out aren't valid.

• Check your sources. We'd like to feel that you wouldn't intentionally post maligning substance on your site, however where you may cause harm is whether you unknowingly source stigmatizing substance and utilization it in your own substance. Make certain you check your sources and inquiry anything that could be viewed as defamatory before you distribute.

Genuine Offender: Many of you presumably recall the prevalent case of online criticism that brought about a $430,000 settlement that Courtney Love paid design originator Simorangkir for the 20 minutes worth of Twitter disdain she unleashed on the architect more than a receipt debate. To her 40,000 devotees, Courtney had called Simorangkir a medication managing, prostitution-pushing hoodlum who lost her youngsters in view of a threatening behavior record.

5. Licensed innovation Laws

Monitors the creation and authorization of protected innovation; For example, copyrights, trademarks, licenses, prized formula laws, and so on. These laws award proprietors particular selective rights to different resources, for example, musical, artistic, and aesthetic works; disclosures and developments; and words, expressions, images, and plans. While Section 230 of the Communications Decency Act does secure you against client created substance that is defamatory, the law does not offer assurance for licensed innovation infringement, importance it is conceivable that you could be discovered obligated if a client presents something on your site that is infringing upon protected innovation laws. Despite the fact that you'll have to reference particular laws to comprehend the intricacies of every, there are a couple of things you can do to verify you remain focused right half of the law.

Instructions to Abide by:

• Attribute your sources. On the off chance that you have any inquiry regarding whether or not (or how) you can utilize another's substance in your own, contact the source. To keep others from utilizing your substance improperly, make an arrangement of substance use/attribution rules (you can allude to Hub Spot's substance utilization rules as a sample), and make them noticeable on your site.

•   Remove faulty client produced substance. Try not to permit content that you believe is disregarding licensed innovation laws to stay on your site. You would prefer not to run the danger of getting sued over it. Make and distribute a client created substance/remarks arrangement that demonstrates you have the privilege to uproot any substance you feel is defamatory, wrong, or disregarding licensed innovation rights and that you will reveal individual data to asking for powers over inquiries of protected innovation infringement.

•   Use Creative Commons-authorized substance. Creative Commons (CC) is a non-benefit association that offers a free different option for full copyright. In advertising, its especially helpful in case you're searching for pictures to use in your substance. The states of CC licenses fluctuate contingent upon which permit the proprietor decided for his/her substance, yet generally, CC-authorized substance can be utilized when credited effectively. This page gives the data you have to know when utilizing/crediting CC-authorized substance. You can likewise economically buy sovereignty free pictures from destinations like iStockphoto, without expecting to plagiarize the source.

Genuine Offender: Who recollects Napster, apparently the most famous protected innovation case ever? Napster permitted clients to share music documents, creating a great many individuals to download tunes free of charge as opposed to obtaining CDs or MP3s. The issue was, Napster didn't possess the rights to the music its clients were transferring to Napster's servers. The Recording Industry Association of America (RIAA) sued Napster and won , driving Napster to close down. Napster is currently claimed by Rhapsody.

6. Revealing Paid Reviews/Promotion/Affiliation

In 2009, the Federal Trade Commission (FTC) distributed modified rules to its FTC Guides Concerning the Use of Endorsements and Testimonials in Advertising. The rules clarify the conditions by which the FTC would discover supports or testimonials unjustifiable or misleading. Per the FTC's rules, a constructive survey from a man associated with the merchant - or somebody who gets money or installment to audit an item or administration - ought to uncover the association between the analyst and the dealer of the item or administration. As it were, bloggers who make an underwriting are obliged to unveil their association with the dealer of the item or administration. Also, if, in a promotion, an organization alludes to the discoveries of an examination association that directed exploration supported by the organization, the advertisement is obliged to uncover the association between the publicist and the analyst. These rules additionally stretch out to casual, under-the-table installments for testimonials from influencers utilized as a part of verbal or buzz advertising.

The most effective method to abide by:

•   Don't ever offer installment in return for positive audits. That said, its consummately worthy to urge clients and fans to abandon you positive audits on the off chance that they wish by reminding your cheerful clients and greatest fans that positive surveys are constantly refreshing.

•   Always unveil associations with accomplices and co-advertising accomplices. Regarding the matter of web promoting, straightforwardness is critical to keeping up a dependable, reliable brand picture.

Genuine Offender: Don't be similar to Legacy Learning Systems, a mainstream vender of guitar-lesson DVDs that wound up with a $250,000 fine for utilizing deceiving online "shopper" and "autonomous" surveys. The FTC charged that it "misleadingly promoted its items through online partner advertisers who dishonestly acted like normal shoppers or free analysts."

CONCLUSION

Copywriting for the web can appear to be verging on overpowering when you stop and take a look at all of the tips and traps important to make an effect on your site. In case you feel like it's too much – don't stress. Like all types of craftsmanship, on the other hand, your copywriting abilities will grow over the long haul – all it takes is practice and the drive to make something exceptional, without fail. Try not to stop now.